THE JOURNEY FROM CREATION TO PROMISE

'The Bridegroom is coming for his Bride'

By Joyce M. Phifer

Copyright © 2017 by Joyce M. Phifer

All rights reserved. All quotations in this book are divinely inspired and therefore written permission must be secured from the publisher to use or reproduce any part of this book, except for brief quotation in critical reviews or articles.

Published in Youngstown, Ohio, by Joyce M. Phifer and distributed in the United States by Joyce M. Phifer, Youngstown, Ohio.

Printed in the United States of America

Scripture quotations, unless otherwise noted, are from the KING JAMES VERSION of the Bible, Copyright © 1979, 1980, 1982, Thompson Chain-Reference Bible, Inc.

ISBN: 978-0-692-88995-4

Phifer, Joyce M.

The Journey From Creation To Promise

DEDICATION

I dedicate this book to my Lord and Savior, Jesus the Christ, for the imparting of His Vision to me in writing it. I also dedicate it to my beloved husband, William L. Phifer Sr. for his patience in understanding my need to give special attention to the writing of this book. Love you to life!

SPECIAL THANKS

I would like to thank Margaret Walker for her illustrations. She captured the vision.

Dr. Mary Bell-Nolan you are a treasure from God. Thanks so much for editing.

Table of Contents

Division One-God in Creation

    Chapter 1-The Gift of life..7

    Chapter 2- Systems for Life..13

    Chapter 3-Why Did God Give Man a Body............................21

    Chapter 4-Why We Need to Repent...23

Division Two-My Concept of an Ancient Jewish Wedding

    Chapter 5-Parental Arrangement..27

    Chapter 6-Bride's Preparation..29

    Chapter7-Groom's Preparation...31

    Chapter 8-Consummation..35

Division Three-My Journey through Life

    Chapter-Birth..37

    Chapter 10-Loss of Momma...43

    Chapter 11-A New Way of living..49

    Chapter 12-The Death of Papa...51

    Chapter 13-Teen Years...53

    Chapter 14-Seeking a Better Life...63

    Chapter 15-Death of My Second Mother................................65

    Chapter 16-A New Lease on Life..71

Chapter 17-A Cry to God for Help..81

Chapter 18-Salvation.. 85

Chapter 19-A Greater Way of Living....................................89

Chapter 20-The Call to Ministry..93

Chapter 21-The Death of my Brother..................................97

Chapter 22-Heartbreaking Ministry...................................101

Division Four-Rapture Season

Chapter23-Come to Jesus..121

Chapter 24-The Greatest Wedding...................................127

Division One-God in Creation

Chapter 1-The Gift of Life

I awakened this morning with sweet thoughts in wonderment of the greatest gift God has given to mankind, the gift of **life**! I imagined God reaching down to the earth, taking the dust from the ground, and meticulously forming the body of Adam. Adam was the only creature that was created by the hands of God. The earth, the waters, the animals were all spoken into existence. Every system that was needed for life with the exception of breath was placed into Adam by the hands of God. God then lovingly bent over the man and breathed into his nostrils according to Genesis 2:7 ***and man became a living soul***. Note: God did not make breath for Adam. God breathed into him, thus he gave Adam his breath. This exchange is what I call 'the great exhale' which is further explained in my booklet "The Great Exhale". God gave Adam breath exclusively from Himself! God exhaled or breathed into Adam's nostrils the breath of life and Adam became a living soul! God resuscitated Adam! But you may ask how could Adam have been resuscitated? Adam had never lived before! I beg to differ with that thought. Adam was with God before the foundation of the world! Jeremiah 1:5a, ***before I formed thee in the belly, I knew thee.*** Ephesians 1:4a, ***according as he hath chosen us in him before the foundation of the world.***

Could it possibly be that you and I lived with God before coming to this earth? Could it be that you and I have been exhaled from God? I dare to believe we were with God before the foundation of the world and yes, he knew you before you were born, he breathed or exhaled the breath of life into each of us and we became living souls.

And God said; Let us make man in our image, after our likeness: And let him have dominion over the fish of the sea, and over the fowl of the air, and over the cattle, and over all the earth, and over every creeping thing that creepeth upon the earth. So God created man in his own image, in the image of God created he him: male and female created he them. And God blessed them, and said unto them, be fruitful and multiply, and replenish the earth and subdue it; and have dominion over the fish of the sea, and over the fowl of the air, and over every living thing that moveth upon the earth. Genesis 1:26-28.

Something special is happening here. God is making man in his own image and God is giving man **dominion** over the fish, the fowl, the cattle and all the earth! Man's dominion extends over all that creeps upon the earth. God never gave dominion to any other creature besides man. To have dominion is to have rule or power over a thing; therefore, **all** creatures are subject to man. Now I understand David's writing of Psalm 8:4-7, '***What is man, that thou art mindful of him? And the son of man that thou visitest him? For thou hast made him a little lower than the angels, and hath crowned him with glory and honor. Thou madest him to have dominion over the works of thy hands: Thou hast put all things under his feet: all sheep and oxen, yea, and the beasts of the field: the fowl of the air, and the fish of the sea, and whatsoever passeth through the paths of the seas.***

So, what is man? Webster defines man as the following:

- A human being; or person
- The human race; mankind

But God has made man a little lower than the angels according to the psalmist. Angels are celestial beings. Angels can inhabit the earth but they are not of the earth. The natural habitat of angels is Heaven. Man on the other hand is terrestrial or of the earth. Man was made to inhabit the earth. Man is considered lower than the angels because his human form limits his ability to dwell with God in Heaven so his connection to God must be spiritual. The spirit of man can travel to Heaven while his physical body must remain on earth.

Everything God made prior to man, God simply spoke those things into existence, but man was special to God, so man was formed in the likeness of God. To form is to mold. When we think of forming something we plan to give it a shape. Now, think of a potter forming a vase or bowl from a lump of clay. The potter must work with the clay until it is of the right consistency. Next, the potter shapes it into his desired height, width or breadth until it is formed into the potter's desired image. We see the potter using his hands to work with the clay until he achieves his desired product. So it was with man, God, the master potter, used his hands to form Adam. Unlike all the other creatures made by God, Adam was formed, and not spoken into existence. *'And the Lord God formed man of the dust of the ground, and breathed into his nostrils the breath of life; and man became a living soul.'* Gen. 2:7 **Below: Illustration of the breath of God entering Adam's nostrils!**

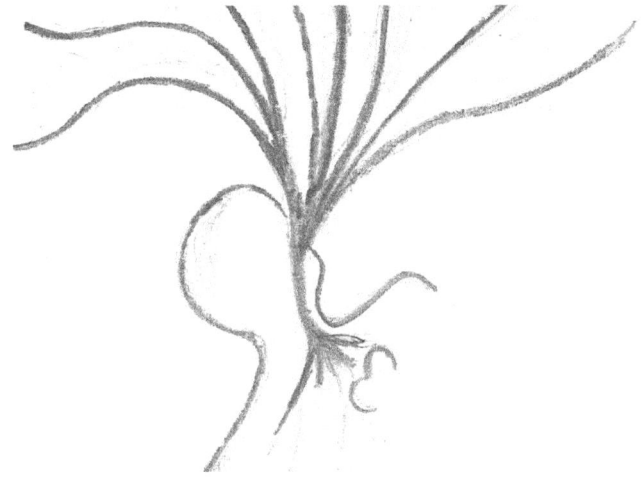

Chapter 2-Systems for Life

Into Adam God placed all of the following systems. Think about the complexity of your body and know you were carefully and lovingly made.

- **A musculoskeletal system**-consists of the human skeleton (which includes bones, ligaments, tendons, and cartilage) and attached muscles. It gives the body basic structure and the ability for movement. In addition to their structural role, the larger bones in the body contain bone marrow, the site of production of blood cells. Also, all bones are major storage sites for calcium and phosphate. This system can be split up into muscular system and the skeletal system.
- **A circulatory system**-this system comprises the heart and blood vessels (arteries, veins, and capillaries). The heart propels the circulation of the blood, which serves as a 'transportation system' to transfer oxygen, fuel, nutrients, waste products, immune cells, and signaling molecules from one part of the body to another. The blood consists of fluid that carries cells in the circulation, including some that move from tissue to blood vessels

and back, as well as the spleen and bone marrow.

- **A digestive system**-consists of the mouth including the tongue and teeth, esophagus, stomach, (gastrointestinal tract, small and large intestines and rectum), as well as the liver, pancreas, gallbladder, and salivary glands. It converts food into small, nutritional, non-toxic molecules for distribution and absorption into the body.
- **An endocrine system**-consists of the principal endocrine glands: the pituitary, thyroid, adrenals, parathyroid, and gonads, but nearly all organs and tissues produce specific endocrine hormones as well. The endocrine hormones serve as signals from one body system to another regarding an enormous array of conditions, and resulting in variety of changes of function.
- **An integumentary system**-consists of the covering of the body (the skin), including hair and nails as well as other functionally important structures such as the sweat glands and sebaceous glands. The skin provides containment, structure, and protection for

other organs, and serves as a major sensory interface with the outside world.
- **A urinary system**-consists of the kidneys, ureters, bladder, and urethra. It removes toxic materials from the blood to produce urine, which carries a variety of waste molecules and excess ions and water out of the body.
- **A nervous system**-consists of the central nervous system, (the brain and spinal cord) and the peripheral nervous system consists of the nerves and ganglia outside of the brain and spinal cord. The brain is the organ of thought, emotion, memory, and sensory processing, and serves many aspects of communication and controls various systems and functions. The special systems consist of vision, hearing, taste, and smell. The eyes, ears, tongue, and nose gather information about the body's environment.
- **A reproductive system**-consists of the gonads and the internal and external sex organs. The reproductive system produces gametes in each sex, a mechanism for their combination, and in the female a nurturing environment for the first nine months of development of the infant.

- **An immune system**-consists of the white blood cells, the thymus, lymph nodes and lymph channels, which are also part of the lymphatic system. The immune system provides a mechanism for the body to distinguish its own cells and tissues from outside cells and substances and to neutralize or destroy the latter by using specialized proteins such as antibodies, cytokines, and toll-like receptors, among many others.
- **A respiratory system**- The respiratory system consists of the nose, nasopharynx, trachea, and lungs. It brings oxygen from the air and excretes carbon dioxide and water back into the air.
- **A Lymphatic system**-Extracts, transports and metabolizes lymph, the fluid found between cells. The lymphatic system is similar to the circulatory system in terms of both its structure and its most basic function, to carry a body fluid. *(definitions of the systems taken from **Wikipedia**, the free dictionary)

Each of these systems is necessary for life. I see God intricately making every part of Adam. Everything had to be perfect. I visualize him putting every strand of hair into place. ***But the very hairs on your head are all numbered.*** Matthew 10:30. I see God placing Adam's eyes the perfect distance apart. Adam's mouth had to be set just right, with the tongue and the teeth perfectly fitting into his mouth. I can see Adam's white teeth gleaming as the sun touched them when he smiled. Adam's nose was shaped to perfection with a nostril on each side. Adam's body was perfectly formed and his organs were made to serve him throughout the ages. The original Adam was built to never know sickness or poor health. Prior to the invasion of sin, God had planned that man would never know death. Man today uses only a small portion of the brain that God has given us. I believe that Adam used all of his. How could he have named all the animals, every creeping thing, and remembered their names without using a full brain? Perhaps I am comparing my brain to Adam's. I have three sons and I am constantly calling them by each other's name. Yes, Adam was crafted by the hands of God, not just designed as an architect designs a building, but literally built by the Master Builder, God.

God placed Adam in a beautiful garden called Eden. God has always prepared a place for us. Everything that Adam needed was in the garden. There was food to eat and water to drink. Adam could eat all the fruit and vegetables he needed to sustain life. The only restriction placed on Adam was that he not eat of the tree of life. Adam even had a job. It was his responsibility to name all the animals, the fowl of the air, the fish of the waters, every beast that existed and every creeping or crawling thing. God saw that Adam was alone and that it was not good so God performed the first surgery by putting Adam to sleep. God took a rib from Adam and with the rib God made Eve. Eve was called woman because she was taken out of the man. Gen. 2:21, 22; **and the Lord caused a deep sleep to fall upon Adam, and he slept, and he took one of his ribs, and closed up the flesh thereof, and the rib, which the Lord God had taken from man, made he a woman, and brought her unto the man.** Eve was taken out of Adam's side to be close to his heart, to be his companion, to be his helpmate, to be his lover, to be his wife. It was the duty of Adam to love her, to protect her and to teach her the ways of God. It was Adam's duty to teach Eve to obey the instructions God had given to Adam in regards to the tree of life. It is the duty of a man today to hear and know the instructions God is giving for his household. It is the responsibility of the woman to accept that God has called the man to be the head or priest of the household especially when the man is following the will and way of God. God never calls two-headed figures but rather calls one to lead and the other to be a help-mate. Does this mean that a woman cannot preach or teach? It certainly does not! It simply means that the man, when in his proper role as the head of the home, is to be a covering for his wife when God has called her to the ministry. God is not a respecter of persons in ministry and he calls and chooses whomever he pleases to perform spiritual assignments. We were created to be temples for God to dwell in enabling us to do his will.

Chapter 3-Why Did God Give Man a Body?

The body of mankind is to be a temple for God to dwell in according to 2 Corinthians 6:16b;' *for ye are the temple of the living God: as God hath said, I will dwell in them; and walk in them; and I will be their God, and they shall be my people.* 'I Corinthians 6:19, 20; *'What? Know ye not that your body is the temple of the Holy Ghost which is in you, which ye have of God and ye are not your own? For ye are bought with a price: therefore glorify God in your body, and in your spirit, which are God's.'* We were born naturally with a prepared body, a body prepared to house God spiritually. We become vessels made ready to become the habitation of the living God. One can become a vessel to house God at any age, young or old. We must be willing to receive him by being 'born again' of the water and the spirit, allowing God to dwell in us. God simply breathes on us and we inhale the Holy Ghost which is evidenced by speaking in 'tongues'. Acts 2:1-4; *and when the day of Pentecost was fully come, they were all with one accord in one place. And suddenly there came a sound from heaven as of a rushing mighty wind, and it filled all the house where they were sitting. And there appeared unto them cloven tongues like as of fire, and it sat upon each of them. And they were filled with the Holy Ghost, and began to speak in other tongues, as the Spirit gave them utterance.* So, what is man? Man is the creature God created before the foundation of the world! Let's take a look at what caused man to fall from his perfect state at creation. It was the sin of disobedience in eating the forbidden fruit by Adam and Eve that caused the separation of God and man. God loved man so much that he sent his only begotten son into the world to die a painful death on a rugged cross shedding his blood so we could be free from sin. God saw us in our sinful state and pitied us. He didn't want us to end up in Hades. He only asks that we believe in him and follow his ways. We must acknowledge that we are sinners and have fallen short of his grace. We begin by with the simple act of repentance. Repentance is imperative for us to enjoy the peace and happiness that comes with living holy. The following steps can lead us to living a holy life beginning with repentance.

Chapter 4-Why We Need To Repent

1. One must first repent in order to begin the walk of a new life in Christ.
2. Repentance is simply acknowledging that you have been living a sin filled life and then making a 180 degree turn from sinful ways to god-like ways.
3. Being baptized in Jesus name for the cleansing of your sins. Acts 2:38-39; **Repent and be baptized every one of you in the name of Jesus Christ for the remission of sins, and ye shall receive the gift of the Holy Ghost. For the promise is unto you and to your children, and to all that are afar off, even as many as the Lord our God shall call.** Why be baptized in the name of Jesus? Acts 4:12, **neither is there salvation in any other; for there is none other name under heaven given among men whereby we must be saved.**
4. The In-filling of the Holy Ghost-the Holy Ghost is the promise Jesus spoke of in John 14:26; **But the comforter, which is the Holy Ghost whom the Father will send in my name, he shall teach you all things, and**

bring all things to your remembrance, whatsoever I have said unto you. Think about what you just read! When you are filled with the Holy Ghost you have Jesus living in you. Everywhere you go, Jesus goes, whatever situation you are in, Jesus is in it with you! You have a problem? You have Jesus the problem solver living in you. Psalm 139:7-10; *whither shall I flee from thy spirit? Or whither shall I flee from thy presence? If I ascend up into Heaven, thou art there: if I make my bed in hell, behold, thou art there, If I take the wings of the morning, and dwell in the uttermost parts of the sea: even there shall thy hand lead me, and thy right hand shall hold me.* We need the Holy Ghost!

Jesus came to the earth to redeem us from sin. He shed his very blood as an offering for you and me. He also said in John 14:1-4; *Let not your heart be troubled: ye believe in God, believe also in me. In my Father's house are many mansions: If it were not so, I would have told you. I go to prepare a place for you. And if I go and prepare a place for you, I will come again, and receive you unto myself; that where I am there ye shall be also. And whither*

I go ye know and the way ye know. When we live for Christ our living is not in vain. He shall come again and bring us to his mansions in the sky! We are all on a journey called life. It sometimes seems that one person's journey has more sadness or tragedy than another's journey. Whatever your life story may be, try to remember our tenure on earth is temporary and not permanent. I will also share my journey with you in a later chapter. Just know our living for Christ is not in vain and see how it relates to an ancient Jewish wedding.

Division Two-My Concept of an Ancient Jewish Wedding

Chapter5-Arrangement by Parents

Let's take a look at an ancient Jewish wedding that would have been performed about the time of Jesus' tenure here on earth. I imagine the prospective groom would have come to the home of she whom he desired to be his bride to obtain permission from her father to marry her. I also imagine this to have been prearranged by their families. The wedding arrangement could have been arranged by the families while the prospective groom and bride were in infancy. The groom would not come empty handed but would come with a substantial gift of at least 50 shekels to present to the father showing she whom he desired was of great worth to him. The groom could be a neighbor or he could have come from a far country, but he had to prove to the father that he had the means by which to take good care of his daughter. Once the father accepted the prospective groom as one worthy to be joined to his daughter in marriage, the maiden was asked if she would accept the marriage proposal. If the maiden accepted, the prospective groom and his intended celebrated by the drinking of a glass of wine together and the father and the groom signed the *ketubbah* which was a contract binding the two in marriage. The signing of the *ketubbah* meant that the bride and groom were legally married but the marriage was not consummated at that time. The groom returned to his home to prepare a place for his soon to be bride while the bride began to prepare herself to leave the home she had always known and prepare herself for her soon returning groom.

In many cases the time of separation was one year and sometimes it was longer depending on the age of the bride at the signing of the *kettubah*. Brides could be chosen at an early age but the marriage could not be consummated until the bride was in her teens. It was the groom's father that decided when the wedding would take place. The groom usually built a room adding it to his father's house in preparation for the soon coming bride. When asked when the wedding would be he would say 'only my father knows'. The groom did not return unto his betrothed until his father said the room is now ready. During this time of preparation the groom would often send gifts to his betrothed showing his love for her.

Chapter 6-Bridal Preparation

So, how did the bride prepare herself for the groom? She prepares herself firstly by beautifying her mind. She probably has dreamed since childhood of one day becoming a bride, now she thinks sweet thoughts of love toward her bridegroom. She thinks of how wonderful it will be to be tenderly embraced in his arms feeling completely safe in his presence. She thinks of his lips sweetly caressing hers. She tries to imagine the passion between them when she surrenders her all to him. She knows she will be his and he will belong to her forever. She is now ready to forfeit all she had before the betrothal. The room that she slept in from childhood no longer will be a place of habitation for her future; it will soon become the bridal chamber. The dolls and toys she once collected have now lost their luster. She would always love her parents and family but recognizes she will soon leave them to be with her bridegroom.

She chooses her bridesmaids, her wedding gown, and her crown. She makes sure her lamps have plenty of oil because she knows not the hour when her beloved will come. If he comes at night her lamps will light her way to him. She now wears a veil whenever in public signifying she is betrothed. She is now committed to her bridegroom and will not allow another to enter her heart. Her mind is now set on her new home, the place her beloved has gone to prepare for her to share with him. The joy of experiencing a new life with her beloved has caused her countenance to change, she is now radiant. She glows with a light that comes from within. This is what she has been waiting for since her youth. She looks forward to the wedding but is in anticipation of the marriage, for then she will feel complete for the rest of her life.

Chapter 7-Groom's Preparation

So what preparations does the groom make during this time of separation? The groom has gone to prepare a home for his bride. It may be that he, too, has always lived at home with his parents and must now add a room to their house for his bride. He not only builds the room but makes sure every detail of the room would be desirable to his bride. He puts fine furniture in place, furniture that oftentimes was crafted by the groom. He purchases fine linens for the bed and beautiful curtains for the windows. A handsome rug was placed on the floor and a fireplace was built to keep his beloved warm during chilly evenings and cold nights. He has his intended in mind as he picks each piece. It is his intention that the home he has picked for her will be better than the home she grew up in.

The time for the wedding has now come. The groom's father has given his approval of the room saying 'it is now ready'. The groom puts on his best apparel and a crown or garland around his head. He sends word to his groomsmen to get ready for the journey. He is now traveling again to the home of his espoused, his intended, his bride. His groomsmen travel with him and at the entrance of her village the shofar is blown to announce his coming. The bride hurriedly gets dressed in her wedding gown with her face covered with her veil and a crown or garland on her head. The bridesmaids scurry around getting their clothing on and shouting 'the bridegroom is coming; the bridegroom is coming! Excitement is in the air.

The father of the bride meets the groom at the door and then they go outside to wait for the bridesmaids and the bride to join them. It seems as if the whole village has gathered outside the house. There is a feeling of great joy and excitement in the air. It is a warm spring night and the moon seems to be shining brighter than ever. One by one the bridesmaids appear in the doorway with their lamps burning to light the way. Each one is arrayed in a beautiful gown. Then the moment that everyone has anticipated happens. The bride appears in the doorway dressed in her beautiful white gown with a garland around her head. The bride comes out to meet the groom. It is night so they have their lamps. The crowd begins to congratulate them as the celebration begins. The bride and groom drink once more a cup of wine. This is the final act of the Jewish wedding. A full goblet of wine is held up and a second goblet of wine is poured, then the wine from each goblet is mixed in a third goblet and the bride and groom drink from this third cup.

Chapter 8 Consummation

In the midst of the celebration the bride and groom slip away into the bridal chamber where they will consummate the marriage. A 'virginity cloth' has been placed on the bed and designated witnesses are outside the room to retrieve the cloth which should be bloody proving the bride was a virgin. The cloth is given to the father of the bride for safe keeping in case the groom wanted to 'divorce' the bride. The groom would not be able to use the grounds that she was not a virgin because the father had proof of his daughter's virginity.

They then travel to the home the groom has prepared. The wedding feast awaits them and they will celebrate sometimes for as many as seven days. As they travel the bride probably looks back on her old home until it fades away. She now turns and looks toward her new home and rejoices in the beauty of it. The new place represents a new beginning, a new life, a new joy, real happiness, and a feeling of security in the love she shares with her bridegroom. She is home at last.

When I think of this Jewish wedding my heart is full of joy because we, the church, are the bride waiting for our groom, the Lord Jesus to appear. Our groom appeared the first time and paid the 'ultimate price' by giving up his life, presenting us with an opportunity of spending eternal life with him. The blood he shed on Calvary caused our sins to be eradicated and we, male and female, become righteous virgins for him by the shedding of his blood. I want to thank you Lord for your precious blood that was shed for mankind. I take it personally; you shed your blood for a wretch like me!

Division Three-My Journey through Life

Chapter 9-Birth

I was born on March 25, 1945 to James Lewis Tellington Jr. and Lucinda Peaks Tellington. My parents married at the tender age of eighteen. My mother's father did not want my mom to marry my dad. He considered my dad to be 'the no-good son' of a Methodist preacher. Someone had to sign the papers giving them permission to marry. Mom told my grandma, whom we called "granny", that she was 'big', which was a term used to indicate the woman was with child. Granny then went to city hall along with my father's grandmother to sign the necessary papers to ensure my parents could be married. My grandfather was not happy about it but did not want my mom to have a baby out of wedlock. Mom had three stillborn babies before I was born, and she and my dad desperately wanted a child. The doctor told mom she would be unable to have a baby. She could conceive but would not be able to carry a child full term, but God had another plan and I was born when mom was twenty-three years of age. Mom said they named me Joyce because of the joy they felt when I was born. Our family grew rapidly and I ended up with two brothers, James and Jerome, and two sisters, Geraldine and Lucille. My daddy had a challenging time keeping a job, so we were underprivileged. I wore second hand clothes, and ate beans with biscuits or cornbread at least three times during the week. My world was perfect just having my mother and father living in the same house.

Soon things changed for us; my daddy would leave for months at a time after losing a job. He was looking for jobs in different cities. My daddy had served time in the army. During his absence, my mom signed up for what was called Soldier's Relief, so that we could eat and have a roof over our heads. If a person received relief, they could only own the minimum necessities. I remember my granny's neighbors moving away and giving mom a black and white floor model television with a tiny screen, and we were ecstatic about it. We had never had a television before but had watched one at a neighbor's house. One of my mom's so called friends became jealous that we had a television. She called the relief office and reported us. A caseworker came out to investigate and mom's check was cut off. She was only allowed a rent voucher and food stamps because it seemed she used money frivolously even though she had not purchased the television. The mere fact that we had the television signified she had obtained it when she didn't have the means to have it.

Regardless of the situation of my father not being there to support us; I loved him dearly. Regardless of the fact that he was an alcoholic; he was still my father. It was my daddy who sat by my bed holding my hand when I was in the hospital with double pneumonia. It was my daddy who cried when I sang a song called "Open the door Richard and let me in"; he was crying because I was saying open the door **Jesus** and let me in. My Parents thought I was going to die; both of my lungs had been affected by pneumonia. God blessed me to recover from the illness. I will never forget the love my father showed me at this critical time in my life.

The first man a girl learns to love is her father, and I adored mine. One of my fondest memories of my daddy was when I was five years old. My mom had gone to the hospital to have my sister Geraldine and daddy had found us a new place to live. It was a nice house with a kitchen that had a big sink and running water. My daddy took me downtown to pick out curtains for the kitchen windows. I felt like a big girl when daddy agreed with my choice. My mom was so surprised and happy when she saw the new place and things went well for us until daddy lost his job. Mom had to go on relief again which meant that daddy could not live in the house, so he left to find another job. We had to move again because mom could not afford the house while on relief. We moved downstairs from my grandparents and papa told mom she should never have married my dad. I loved my mother's father who I affectionately called "papa" but hated to hear him say anything negative about my father.

My daddy would come home in the middle of the night to visit mom and sometimes I would wake up and see him. My parents made me promise to never tell anyone daddy had been there, not even my siblings. Soon my mother was 'big' again with my brother Jerome, and one year later with my youngest sister Lucille. Papa was furious with my daddy and even threatened to hurt him for ruining mom's life. My mom applied for an apartment in a new development called the projects. We moved there when I was ten years old. Papa and granny had moved there about a year earlier, and we had been on a waiting list for a three-bedroom apartment which would be large enough for the six of us, my mom, my two brothers and two sisters, and me. We were forced to take a two-bedroom apartment and the girls and I shared our mom's bedroom. Things were looking up for us, we had a roof over our head, food and clothing, a nice place to live, but something was missing, my daddy had not come to visit for a long time.

Chapter10-The Loss of Mom

In July of 1957 my daddy wrote mom saying he had found a good job in Detroit, Michigan at one of the factories there. He was making preparations to relocate our family to Detroit. I remember the last time we spoke to him from a phone in a telephone booth. Mom seemed happy but apprehensive about us moving. It was now August of that year and I was to enter junior high school that September. I had mixed emotions about moving and leaving my friends but was happy to know we were going to be a real family again.

I woke up early on August 24, 1957; it was a beautiful summer day and mom was not feeling well. She asked me to fix my siblings' breakfast. After breakfast I did the ironing of the pillowcases and other clothing my mother had separated for me to iron. The day passed quickly with me caring for the kids and soon it was time for the show 'Gunsmoke', starring Matt Dillon to come on television. Mom called my brother James and me to come to her room. She said to us, 'I am not going to be here with you always, but I want you to look out for the younger kids and each other'. We said "yes ma'am" without really knowing what she meant. We just wanted to get back into the front room and watch 'Gunsmoke'. Soon after leaving the room we heard a loud thump as my mother fell out of bed and hit her head on a bucket. She had asked me to bring the bucket into the room earlier so she could spit into it. She was foaming at the mouth and she did not answer me when I asked what happened. We didn't have a phone, so I went to a neighbor's apartment and called an ambulance and my mother's sister, Aunt Mae, who told me to get the other kids dressed and take them to a cousin's house that was in walking distance. She also told me which hospital to have the ambulance take my mother to.

We went to my Cousin Fanny's house after the ambulance left with my mother. Fanny had two sons that were older than me so she left for the hospital leaving us in the older son's care. We played a card game called 'war' to pass the time and then I heard a small voice saying 'your mother is not coming back', she has died'. I told my brother James what I had heard and he started crying saying it was not true. It was now before day on August 25, 1957 and my Aunt Mae and my Cousin Fanny came into the house crying. They said my mother had died. They said the doctors had tried to help her by putting a tube into her mouth, but she kept pushing it away until she died. They said it was like she didn't want to live. This description was too much for me at age twelve to handle. I couldn't even cry. I guess I was in shock. How would we live without the stabilizing presence of our mother?

My mother was a woman of prayer. I would hear her in the middle of the night calling out to God for help in providing for her children. She referred to him as her way maker, her doctor, her lawyer and her provider. She also knew him as a very present help. My mother's death took away my trust in this God whom she referred to as being a God of love. It seemed to me that a God who loved me would never leave me defenseless and homeless by taking my mother. My mother took us to church, helped us with our homework, and helped me study for the spelling bee. I won the spelling bee at my school in grades 4, 5, and 6. I was an A & B student and my mom always showered me with praise for my accomplishments. Now she was gone! Who would take us in? I was filled with bitterness and had lost faith in God. I didn't believe I could trust him. My mother must have prayed prayers to God to keep us during that time because I soon began to enjoy going to church and worshipping God again. I can remember thanking him for not allowing her to suffer. Mom's death was sudden and unexpected.

My aunt notified her sisters, my Aunt Frances and Aunt Lucille who lived in Detroit that my mother had died. My Aunt Frances told my father. Daddy will come and get us just as he and mom had planned and we would live with him in Detroit I thought. The day of the funeral came and daddy still had not come. I stared at the casket but could not cry. My sister Lucille kept crying and asking me to wake up mom so we could go home. Lucille was only three years old. I tried to comfort my sister but I think I was still in a state of shock. What will we do now?

We were staying temporarily with my Aunt Mae who lived on the Southside of Youngstown. The family began to make arrangement for where we would live. They had decided we were to be separated and live with different relatives. I remembered what mom had said before she died about us looking out for each other and our younger siblings. Here we were five children, ages 12, 10, 7, 5, and 3 years of age. Lucille would turn 4 in September. We were too young to be on our own and I didn't want us to be separated. I was afraid the younger ones would forget our family and they probably would even forget mom.

I knew how to cook, wash, iron and clean a house. My mom taught me those things at a young age. She often put me in charge of the younger ones; whenever she had to be away from us to shop or tend to business. I went to my Aunt Mae when I learned we were to be separated and asked her to keep us together and I would do all the necessary things to help her with my siblings. I thought I must have been very convincing because she agreed to keep us all. Now I realize that God in his infinite wisdom and mercy had already made a way for us and that is the real reason she consented to keep us. Also, I realize what a tremendous sacrifice I had asked of her. She had recently remarried after the death of her first husband. The wonderment of it all was that her new husband agreed to take us in permanently. The miracle in this arrangement was that my daddy and this man had fought some years earlier while drinking, and my dad had slit this man's throat just missing the jugular vein. God touched this man's heart with compassion for us kids and he took us in.

Chapter11-A New Way of Living

My aunt's two older daughters stayed with her from time to time plus she had a seven year old daughter and two granddaughters from a daughter that was deceased. My new uncle, who we called Uncle R, also had two sons and two daughters that came to live with us shortly after they took us in. Uncle R's children had been living with his oldest daughter in Chicago since the death of his first wife. Uncle R wanted them to live with him since he had a new wife to help him care for them.

Living with Aunt Mae and Uncle R was quite an adventure. The one day of the week that remained consistent was Sunday; all of us kids had to go to Sunday school and church. We would awaken to the sounds of church songs playing on the record player. Uncle R might get drunk every other day of the week but on Sundays he played church songs while he fried chickens taken from his hen house and cooked greens from his garden. Every now and then he would even bake 'tea cakes' for us kids. I will be eternally grateful to Aunt Mae and Uncle R for rescuing us and allowing us to grow up together.

We went to a little Baptist church with very few adult members but lots of kids from the community. The pastor only baptized in the summer months because we didn't have a baptismal pool in our small church and I was designated the pastor's helper. It was my responsibility to lead my younger siblings, my cousins and all the baptismal candidates out to the water of Mosquito Lake, to the pastor, to be baptized. I didn't realize it at the time, but this was the beginning of ministry for me.

Chapter 12-The Death of Papa

Things happen in strange ways. My papa died two months to the day my mother passed. He died on October 25, 1957. Granny didn't want us to tell him my mom had died because he had already become listless and remained in bed all day long. Two days after mom died papa asked to see me. He was use to my coming to visit them every day during the summer months. Our apartments were a couple of blocks away from each other and I would visit them daily. I think papa felt something was wrong and my not coming to visit made him wonder what it could be. My aunt took me to my grandparent's apartment and warned me not to let papa know that momma had died. Mom was only thirty four years old and the youngest of his children. Papa said she was a preemie and they brought her from the south in a boot box because she was so small. The family thought he would not survive if he knew mom was dead.

I drudgingly entered papa's bedroom and the first thing he asked was 'where is your momma'? Before I could answer he said, 'don't lie to me Joyce, I know they're trying to keep it from me'! Cindy's dead isn't she? I broke down into tears and didn't answer him.

I couldn't stand the hurt look on his face. Granny came into the room and told papa not to make me cry. I then said, yes, papa, mom is dead! Papa couldn't attend the funeral and he started going downhill rapidly. He spent his last week in the hospital where I visited him as often as I could. He had to have oxygen and at that time they put a mask over your mouth and nose. Papa kept trying to take the mask off. He seemed ready to die. Papa had been a gardener for the doctor who took care of him. I never knew papa's age, but the doctor said he had to be over 100 years of age. The medicine the doctor was giving him had no effect on his body.

Chapter13-Teen Years

The next few years went by quickly. I put up my age to get babysitting jobs to help support my siblings. I went to school, but soon lost interest because it seemed that no one cared if I accomplished anything. I hated going to school on Thursdays while in junior high because the school was across the street from where we lived and the police were called to the house to break up a fight between family members who had been drinking just about every payday. It was embarrassing because my classmates knew the police were at the house I lived in and they laughed and teased me constantly.

I entered high school and things were a little better. I was now a C student just doing enough to get by. A new man named Fred moved across the street from us. He and his uncles made moonshine and they became friends with my family right away. I was fifteen years old and Fred payed me a lot of attention, when he saw me walking up the street he would get into his car and follow me trying to get me to get into the car with him. At first I ignored him but someone saw me talking to him and told my aunt I was sneaking around with him. I tried to explain but was called a liar. I couldn't leave the house without him seeing me and he continued to follow me.

I was accused over and over about sneaking to see Fred, who was nine years older than me! I soon became weary of the accusations and decided if I were being accused of seeing him I might as well do it. I then began to sneak around with him. **Life lesson**: Never allow another's accusations to cause you to do something you know is wrong. When we allow other's opinions to steer us, it is our own ego that is leading us. I was awed by the thought that an older man could be interested in me and this lead to my demise.

It was Christmas Day 1961 and my aunts from Detroit had come home to spend the holidays with the family. My Aunt Frances spent Christmas night with my Cousin Marie who lived up the street from us. Aunt Frances became ill on Christmas Day, was taken to the hospital and was released with the diagnosis of having heartburn. It was about 1 am on the morning of December 26th when Marie called her mom, my Aunt Mae, to say something was wrong with my Aunt Frances. Aunt Mae woke me up to go to Marie's house to see what was wrong. I arrived at the house and Marie met me at the door and handed me a small mirror saying 'take this upstairs and put it in front of Aunt Frances' nose to see if she is breathing'. I did as she asked and came back downstairs to say, 'Aunt Frances is not breathing, I believe she is dead'. Marie called an ambulance and they took my aunt to the hospital. Aunt Frances had died of a heart attack. Aunt Frances had no children. She had wanted to rear all five of us kids when because she was not married.

I was devastated at the death of this aunt. It seemed God was still taking away from me the people I loved. I had been a good girl up until then but decided death would take away everything anyway so I might as well enjoy whatever time I had on earth. I had not slept with Fred even though he had asked me to on several occasions. It would be New Year's Eve soon and I made a plan to sleep with Fred on New Year's Eve. Yes, I was the one who made the plan to sleep with him. Sometimes we make decisions that alter our lives in a negative way and we want to blame someone else for those decisions. I was only sixteen but would be seventeen in three months. I told my aunt I would be babysitting overnight and my employer would pick me up after choir rehearsal. I packed a bag and went to choir rehearsal. Fred picked me up at the church and kept asking if I were sure I wanted to do this. We went to a motel and after making sure I was settled in the room, Fred left saying he had to make a run. I think He was having second thoughts about sleeping with me. He was gone so long that I began to cry thinking he had just left me there. He later came back and we had sex. I use the word sex because it was a terrible experience for me. Emotionally I was not ready for sex. I was looking for what I saw on television, the romance, the flowers and all the tender embraces. My body was not ready for this experience either.

I had no period in January and by February I knew I was pregnant. Fred and I had not slept together since that night. I told him I was pregnant and by then I knew I didn't want to be with him so I asked him for money so I could go to My Aunt Lucille's in Detroit and he seemed happy that this might solve his problem of having to care for me. Meanwhile I confided in my Cousin Beatrice, Uncle R's daughter, and she told another cousin who suggested I have an abortion. This cousin was really trying to help me out of my situation but I believed to abort was to murder so I wanted no part in that. I hated to leave my siblings but thought I could find our father and get him to take us all in. It seemed all my life I was searching for security and help from my earthly father without knowing it was my heavenly father and a relationship with him was what I really was longing for. I didn't find what I needed in my natural father or in my relationship with Fred.

I arrived in Detroit and took a cab to my aunt's house. She was not happy to see me and said I would have to go back home. She did take me to see my daddy who was living in a horrible place that was not clean and he didn't have a job. He took one look at me and said, 'you're pregnant aren't you?' He said he couldn't help me and he, too, said I should go back home. His advice to me was to read Psalm 27:10 and believe what it said. **When my father and my mother forsake me, then the Lord will take me up.** God promises to never leave me or forsake me. My earthly father had not only removed his presence from me but he had left me emotionally also. My daddy's true emotions were tied to the bottle; he had the illness of alcoholism. I was devastated by his words because he had always been my hero. I truly believe my daddy in his own way was trying to convey to me that I must not trust in man alone because man will forsake you but I could trust in God who would never forsake me. I now thank him for giving me this psalm. This psalm means much to me because I later came to the realization that God really does take us up and God becomes everything we need him to be. The last words my father spoke to me as I was preparing to leave were these. 'Joyce, don't marry the man you love, marry a man who loves you even if you don't love him in the beginning. You will learn to love him!' That was the last time I would ever hear my daddy speak to me. I left that place torn in my emotions; it hurt to see him living in a place of disarray and yet I felt completely dismayed that he didn't make any attempt to help me.

My Aunt Lucille gave me cab fare to the bus station and what she thought was enough money for the bus ticket. I went to purchase the ticket but was short of the purchase price, I didn't know what to do. I couldn't call my Aunt Lucille because she didn't have a phone. I began to pray and ask God to help me. I was still a teenager and I felt completely alone and helpless. I was afraid to talk to anyone in that enormous bus station and then I saw a man in clergy clothes coming my way. I stopped him and explained my dilemma. He went to the window with me and added the amount of money I needed for the ticket. I turned to say thank you but he had disappeared. I believe the man was an angel! I could see quite far in either direction from where I was standing and he was not to be seen anywhere. Again, this God I wanted to hate had sent me help. ***God is our refuge and strength a very present help in trouble.*** Psalms 46:1.

I arrived in Youngstown and was picked up from the bus station by my cousin Mary and her boyfriend. They took me to their apartment where I stayed until my baby was born. Fred found out I was back and he tried to help me financially. My baby boy who I called Larry was born on September 17, 1962. He would have been taken away from me if Mary had not intervened by saying she would supervise the baby's care. I had turned seventeen that March but was underage to rear a child. The night our child was born Fred was picked up for 'moonshining' which was a federal offense. The baby was a week old before he saw him the first time. He went to court and was given three years in a federal prison. We wrote to each other often and then came the day he was released. I was committed to having a relationship with him and to marriage. I wanted my child to have his father in his life. We made plans to marry and he took me to North Carolina to meet his father. I found out while there that he had a wife and three kids; was not divorced, and I was devastated. He said he didn't know how to tell me and the news really came as a shock. I was sick during the entire visit and found out later that I was pregnant with our second child, a son he named Coya. I had spent four years of my life waiting for a man who was already married!

Fred had surgery soon after our baby was born and was laid up for a short time. We had an agreement that we would stay together until Christmas and then he would move out. He said he owed it to me and the boys to give us a good Christmas.

Fred had gotten another girl pregnant and her baby was born in 1962 also, somewhere around the time our first child was born. The girl was younger than me and the baby was taken from her. She knew he was out of prison and where we lived and sent a young man to our door looking for him. I told the young man he was recuperating and could not come to the door. Soon after, I heard a woman screaming his name. It was the young woman he had impregnated. I asked her to leave from my door and she did. The poor girl was drunk. The next day I took all his clothes and thru them on her porch after finding out where she lived from his brother. I didn't want to wait until Christmas; I felt I had been through enough. The girl came to her door and apologized to me saying she was sorry and that she had too much to drink. I walked away leaving his clothes behind. Fred did everything he could to make amends. I had no job or way of taking care of myself and my kids so I let him back in. I didn't let him know I was applying for welfare. I saved up enough money to move. Fred kept his word and gave us a beautiful Christmas and unbeknown to me he had already picked out my replacement and gave her and her children a nice Christmas too.

Chapter 14-Seeking a Better Life

I moved in January leaving Fred's clothes in the apartment. Later he told me he had a terrible feeling as he pulled up to the apartment after work and the blinds were down. It was about 3:30 in the afternoon and I always had the blinds up in the daytime.

I refused to be intimate with him. It wasn't that I hated him; I hated myself for putting myself in the predicament I was in. I was very lonely but knew I couldn't continue to live as I had in the past. There was a day when loneliness almost overtook me. I turned on the oven and didn't light it. I lay on the couch with my children near me. I just wanted to go to sleep and not wake up to the issues of life. The thought came to me that it was unfair to end the children's lives just because I was miserable about the mess mine was in. I got up, turned the oven off and aired the house. I would go on and suffer whatever consequences came my way. **Suicide is never the answer regardless of the problem!**

Fred would come by to see the boys or take them for a ride but I wouldn't let him touch me. He started parking outside of my house late at night and playing his music and I would wake up, look out the window and see him. It took everything good that was left within me to keep from opening my door to him. One day he stopped by supposedly on his way to the cleaners and brought some of his clothes into my house. I literally freaked out! I told him to put those clothes back into his car! I didn't want anything of his in my house. I was determined to not get trapped again. I made a vow to myself that I would rear my children alone. I didn't even date!

Chapter 15-Death of My Second Mother

In January of 1968 my Aunt Mae became ill and was taken to the hospital. I had no car so I had to rely on Fred to take me back and forth to the hospital. I received a call from Mary saying 'if you want to see your aunt before she dies you need to get to the hospital, the doctor has given her three days to live'. I immediately called Fred and he picked me and the boys up and we went to the hospital. Mary was in the hall crying and said, 'you're too late, she's gone'. I went into the room to say goodbye to my aunt, my second mother, who was now dead! I was truly shaken up. I couldn't stop crying. Fred stopped at the liquor store and bought some gin before taking me home. He encouraged me to drink what he called a tonic to settle my nerves. He must have fed the kids and put them to bed because I didn't wake up until the next morning and there he was in bed with me. My aunt died on January 19, 1968 and on October 9, 1968 our third son Anthony was born.

I was almost 23 years old, unmarried with two children and pregnant with the third. I wanted to get custody of my three younger siblings. I didn't have to worry about my brother James because he would be turning twenty-one in April. Again, God made a way for us. I was living in a two bedroom house and would need a four bedroom house to accommodate us. I had made friends with an Italian woman who lived up the street from me in a four bedroom house with beautiful drapes and carpets. This woman's husband was being transferred to a job in another city and she offered to rent me her house at the same price I was paying for the two bedroom house. I accepted her offer, moved into the house and petitioned the court for custody of my siblings. The court did an investigation and I was awarded custody. This, too, was a set-up from God. The woman and her husband wanted to move back into the house in less than three months! Something had gone wrong with the job transfer. God had given me that beautiful house for the space of time I would need to get custody of my siblings! **God may not come when you want him to but he never comes late. He really is an on time God!** I then moved into a duplex on the east side of town. It was an okay house but nowhere near as nice as the one I moved from.

Fred was living with a pretty lady he had brought from the south and she knew about me and the boys but he didn't want her to know he had slept with me again. When I told him I was pregnant he looked me in the eye and said, 'the baby can't be mine'. Those words pierced my very soul. He couldn't have hurt me more if he had taken a gun and shot me! Somehow I mustered up enough courage to say, 'you can deny being the father, but I will be the child's mother'! Fred didn't come around until after the baby was born, and I didn't call him or ask him for anything. He showed up when the baby was about a month old trying to apologize and when he touched me by putting his hand on my shoulder; it seemed as if my skin recoiled. **Hatred** boiled up in me and I asked him to leave and not come back. **Hatred is like cancer! It doesn't harm the person it's directed to but can damage or destroy the person carrying it emotionally and physically!** I felt rejected, overwhelmed and dismayed. How could this be happening to me? I asked God to release hatred in me for my children's sake. I didn't realize it at the time but I needed the release for my own sake! Fred would always be a part of my life because of the children even though I didn't want him around. I also had to forgive him, but unfortunately forgiveness didn't happen until years later. I wanted revenge for Fred saying the baby was not his and when he would come to pick the boys up I wouldn't allow the baby boy to go with them. I didn't recognize it then but I was hurting Tony by not allowing him to be a part of his father's life. He was well loved by my husband as were the other children but felt he had no natural father. It was only after he was grown that I found this out and Fred and I sat him down and explained that my actions had been because of words he said when we were young and they were then able to have a relationship together.

My desire for revenge had done great harm to my son. Outwardly he seemed happy but being unsure of his parentage caused him to have a feeling of not really belonging. Revenge can damage innocent victims! Oh the webs that we do weave when first we practice to deceive.

I had taken a test to enter practical nursing school in the spring but I would no longer be accepted because I was pregnant. The school in my city was full but I would have been able to move to Salem, Ohio and enter school there. The program provided an apartment and a daycare for my two boys. Even though I had passed the test I would have to put my desire for betterment on hold while I reared my boys and helped my siblings. I have often wondered whether or not I would have made the decision to help my siblings if I had not had children of my own.

Chapter 16-A New Lease on Life

A strange thing happened when I was about six months pregnant with Anthony. A car pulled up and parked in front of the duplex where I lived. A man and a woman got out of the car. I recognized the woman and knew she was a friend of my neighbor's but I didn't recognize the man. They walked up the steps towards me and I told them they were on the wrong side of the duplex. The woman continued towards the neighbor's side but the man stopped, looked at me and said, 'I'm going to marry you'. Well, I had a few choice words for him; but he just smiled and continued into my neighbor's house. I forgot about the incident but a few weeks later he came back and asked my sister if I was home. I just happened to be away but when told he had been there I instructed my family to always tell him I was not home.

This man, whose name was William Phifer, was persistent and continued to come by for months. He was tall, thin and nice looking. I was attracted to him but determined I was not going to be misused by another man. I just wanted to rear my boys and see to it that my siblings were taken care of. One day he came by while one of my younger cousins was visiting, he knocked on the door and when I looked out the window and saw it was him I gave my cousin instructions to answer the door and say I was not home. She answered the door saying, 'she said she's not home'. I thought he would stop coming after realizing I really was home; but this didn't deter him. It was as if he was on a mission to disrupt my life and I wanted no part of it. I told granny about him and she said she would like to meet him and as fate would have it he came by on Thanksgiving Day while granny was there having dinner with us. He knocked on the door and granny said let him in. He came in and introduced himself to my family. He and my granny talked for hours. Granny told me after he left that she felt he was a good man. 'Joyce, you're too young to give up on having a good relationship. You should give him a try.' I grew up thinking granny was my natural grandmother; I found out after the death of papa that she was papa's second wife and had helped him raise my mother and her siblings after the death of his first wife. Granny was the same age as my Aunt Mae! She always treated us as if we were of her bloodline and I not only loved her but trusted in her wisdom.

I heard what granny said but I couldn't trust myself. I was afraid loneliness would cause me to make another mistake. I worked afternoons cleaning offices and when William found out where I worked he showed up there to take me home. I refused the ride and went home with my regular ride. He would show up at least once a week. He contacted my granny and asked her how to get my attention. My granny told him to stop by the house and pick up my kids, she would arrange for my sister to have them ready and I would have to accept his ride because my children were in the car. This act between my granny, my sister and my soon to be husband sparked the beginning of a relationship. We dated for a short time and later married. He often reminds me that I turned him into a stalker. He said he didn't know why he proposed marriage when seeing me for the first time but believes it was a God-thing.

Marriage to William started out wonderfully. He was a good father to the children and a considerate, sometimes doting, husband to me. God had set me up to be a wife to this patient, loving man. We talked for hours at a time. William was born in Youngstown but his family moved to Omaha, Nebraska when he was thirteen years old. He had an older sister and brother which made him the baby of the family. William's entire family died within a two year period. William's father died in April of 1949 from tuberculosis, his mother died in June of 1949 from a massive heart attack, his sister died in September of 1949 of tuberculosis and his brother died in 1951 from tuberculosis. God spared William. He never had symptoms of that deadly disease which took the lives of many people during that era. William and I had a lot in common. We had both lost loved ones at an early age and we both were looking for love. I like to think God spared him for me. William returned to Youngstown at the age of nineteen to live with his father's sister and her family. He said he was looking for a wife who would love him. Loving William was the best thing that ever happened to me save Jesus. The thirteen year difference in our age didn't seem to matter. Perhaps it was the hardships I faced in life which made me appear to be older than my years. William didn't look or act his age. I actually thought he was my age until he told me the ages of his children.

William was married prior to meeting me and had three almost grown children, a son that was seven and three step-children from his marriage. We did our best to try to make each of them feel included in our family. When you adopt children you can become their mother. When you become part of a union where the children of your spouse have a loving mother and you are eight years older than your spouse's oldest natural daughter, and a few years older than his step-daughter, the best you can hope for is to be friends, yet, let them know your door is always open.

By August of 1972 all my siblings had married and moved out of our house. William was instrumental in securing jobs with the railroad for both of my brothers. William and I had a good relationship. He didn't want me to work outside the home but I felt we could buy a house sooner if he would let me work. This was a bad decision on my part and it almost destroyed our marriage. **One must take time to find what your intended's needs are before you marry and do your best to honor them!** William had grown up in a home where his dad worked and took care of all the finances and his mother was a full time housewife. William had always envisioned himself as the provider and being a housewife was what he wanted from me. I on the other hand wanted more for us. I also wanted more for the children. I wanted them to go to private school and then college. We would not be able to do those things without a second income. William reluctantly relented and I became employed at a car factory.

We bought our first home in June of 1975. There were now five children in the house full time and William's baby boy, Roy, made six because he spent his summers and weekends with us. We tried to make his place in our home special by telling him he was the youngest of the first set of children and the elder of the second set. Two daughters had been added to our family, our daughter Monique was born in 1970 and Michelle was born in 1971. The six children got along very well and enjoyed each other's company.

My job at the car factory brought in a good income but my marriage was falling apart. William had begun to drink heavily because he was miserable with our arrangement. He worked day turn and I worked afternoons. I wanted to quit work and go back to our original agreement of my only working for six months but was afraid to because he was missing so much work due to his drinking. I now had the house I wanted but it seemed that my marriage would end if something didn't change. It was even hard for us to communicate with each other and soon our conversations were only about the kids or bills that were due.

William hated the fact that alcohol was taking over his life and helping to destroy our marriage so he signed himself into a clinic for alcoholics. He was diagnosed there as being in the early stages of cirrhosis of the liver. While William was in the clinic, my brother James came home from work and found a note from the police department saying that our father was in the hospital and unresponsive. The note didn't give any details and when we called the police station for more info no one there knew anything about the note. **Could an angel have placed the note on my brother's door?** I decided to call the hospitals in Detroit to see if I could find our father. You had to pay for long distance calls at that time and I was connected to a compassionate operator. I told her my dad was in a Detroit hospital, I didn't know which one, but I needed to find out in order to go see him. She asked his name which is the same as my brother's and she put me on hold while she contacted the different hospitals. She found the right hospital and gave me the information and I was never charged for the calls. **This was another set-up**

from God. She then connected me to the hospital. I talked with the nurse and let her know we had just found out our father was hospitalized but would be there to see daddy on Saturday. We sometimes pray prayers and forget what we have prayed. My prayer had been, God don't let my father die without me seeing him again. I contacted the clinic and had my husband released so he could accompany me to Detroit.

We arrived in Detroit on Saturday morning and went straight to the hospital. We came to a ward and I stopped because I could see a man curled up in a fetal position while lying in bed that looked like my dad. We entered the room and sure enough it was daddy. He was unresponsive when talking to him but as I moved around the room he seemed to follow me with his eyes. He just stared at us and never said a word. The nurse entered into the room and said he had been there since August and it was now October. My mind went back to a night in August when I felt someone tugging at my feet. I woke my husband up asking him why he was tugging at my feet and he said he had not touched my feet. I went back to sleep but the incident stayed with me. Could I have been awakened at the time my father was having the traumatic experience which caused him to be hospitalized? The nurse watched his eyes as he tried to follow our movement in the room and said he had not been this responsive since entering the hospital in August. We returned to the hospital on Sunday, Oct. 6, spent the day with daddy and left the hospital for home after giving the nurse our contact information and saying we would be back the next weekend.

Wednesday, Oct. 9, was Tony's birthday and I left for work late after celebrating with the family. I arrived at the plant and the workers were leaving, there had been a fire in one of the departments and the plant was being shut down for the night. I got back into my car and as I was driving down the highway I had an uneasy feeling of someone watching me. I arrived home and the feeling of uneasiness was still with me. I decided to go to bed and when I reached the top of the stairs I heard a sound like chains being dragged across the hardwood floor downstairs. I didn't know what it was but I started to throw shoes down the stairs in hopes of scaring away whatever was making the noise. Later, my husband came in and wanted to know why all those shoes were on the floor downstairs and I told him what I heard.

The next morning my sister called to say the hospital had called her saying our father had passed the night before. God had answered my prayer of seeing him before he died! I can't explain the uneasiness of feeling eyes on me while driving home that night, nor can I explain the sound of chains going across the floor. I will probably never have the answer to those events. We traveled again to Detroit to make arrangements for our father's burial. This was the first time I ever had to make arrangements for a funeral and when I entered the room to pick out the casket I nearly fainted.

My husband was very supportive of me during my time of bereavement but was still drinking heavily and he had started gambling. Things had gotten so bad I had to ask the payroll clerk at his job not to give him his paycheck for fear he would gamble it all away. Life's events were taking a toll on me.

Chapter 17-A Call to God for Help

I was devastated and very depressed. I lost quite a bit of weight and my blood pressure was out of control. I felt completely hopeless. Somehow in my past I had been able to control most of the events in my life in one way or another; but I was completely helpless in fixing my marriage. One weekend after putting the kids to bed I fell to my knees in my upstairs hallway and cried out to God. Please help me; I can't live like this any longer. I need your help God! Please show me what to do! **This poor man cried, and the Lord heard him and saved him out of all his troubles.** Psalm 34:6. As I fell to my knees it was as if I could feel hands wrapping around me; I felt an assurance that everything would be alright. I believe God had been waiting on me to ask for his help. I really missed my husband; the tender moments and the wonderful times we shared in the past. I wanted it back but didn't know how to get it. I went to work the next week still heavy hearted and when my relief man came to give me a break God gave me an answer to my problems.

My relief man, whose name is Sam, had a foul mouth and I hated conversing with him as he relieved the person before me and then relieved the person after me. Something was different about Sam that night. He appeared to have a glow on his face and he didn't use one derogative when talking to me on the break before lunch. Lunch came and went and Sam was still smiling with a glow on his countenance. After my break I said to him, there is something different about you Sam, what is it? He smiled and said, 'I thought you'd never ask! I've been baptized in Jesus name and filled with the Holy Ghost! I knew about the Holy Ghost because Uncle R had a sister and a niece who would come to the house from time to time trying to get the family saved. I was a young teen then and laughed to myself whenever I heard them speak in what they called 'tongues' not knowing one day, I too, would speak in tongues or an unknown language. I asked Sam to explain to me what happened to him. He had gone to church with a member of a Bible class I attended during lunch there at the plant. I later found out I had never been invited to this church because the members thought I was already saved because of the way I carried myself.

I thought about the difference in Sam and I wanted to have the peace and joy I could see on his face. Sam had been dealing with a wife who was very ill and normally he would be complaining about the struggles of caring for her and his family. Receiving the Holy Ghost had brought about a change in him and it showed outwardly. I went home thinking I would let the group know the next day that I wanted to be baptized even though I had been baptized a few months after the death of my mother; I knew I needed something more.

Chapter 18-Salvation

I woke up early the next morning and began to clean the house after sending the kids off to school. My youngest had not entered kindergarten yet so she was home with me. I was a smoker and decided I would not smoke anymore. I was going to work and planned to tell the Bible class group I wanted to be baptized. I had a full pack of cigarettes and an open pack with maybe five cigarettes in it. I twisted the open pack and threw it and the full pack into an empty waste basket and got dressed for work. My baby girl came after me as I was leaving saying, 'mommy you forgot your cigarettes'! I looked at the pack I had twisted and it was now straight! I thanked my baby and walked out the door with tears in my eyes knowing I had twisted those cigarettes. I cried most of the thirty minutes it took to drive to work. One moment I was thinking of being baptized and the next moment I was thinking I didn't need to because I had been baptized before. I thought I had convinced myself to not be baptized when I met one of the Bible group members as I entered the plant. I blurted out to him that I wanted to be baptized and he said he would make arrangements for someone to meet us at the church after work that night. Mt.

Calvary believed in opening its doors for baptism whenever a person wanted to be baptized. It didn't matter what time it was, a minister and helpers were on call to baptize you.

I left work and headed for the church. I was met there by two women, and the preacher who baptized me. Three men from the Bible class came also. The women dressed me in baptismal clothing and helped me up the steps to the baptismal pool. I remember the preacher saying, **'my dear sister, according to your faith and the confidence you have in the word of God, concerning his birth, death, and resurrection, I now baptize you in the name of the Lord Jesus Christ for the remission of your sins and you shall receive the gift of the Holy Ghost'**. I thought to myself, he has baptized me wrong. He should have said in the name of the Father, and of the Son and the Holy Ghost. It wasn't too long afterwards that I learned of the oneness of God. **Hear O Israel the Lord our God is one**. I felt clean as I dried off and soon I was kneeling at the altar of that beautiful church called Mount Calvary Pentecostal Church. The date was January 23, 1976. Someone told me to start praising God and soon I heard a voice speaking in a beautiful strange language. I opened my eyes to see who was speaking. The men who came with me were rolling on the floor and the women were rejoicing and I realized it was me speaking! I came to church a little before midnight and I lost track of time because I was caught up in talking to God. One of the women became weary around daybreak and stopped me from speaking. She read Acts 2:38, **then Peter said unto them, repent and be baptized every one of you in the name of Jesus Christ, for the remission of sins and ye shall receive the gift of the Holy Ghost.** I've repented and I've received the Holy Ghost, I said. How do you know? She asked. I heard myself speaking in another language I answered. Repentance was not hard for me; I knew I had lived life contrary to God's will. I had to believe God had forgiven me and I also had to forgive myself. I left for home feeling good about my experience and thanking God for saving a wretch like me.

I hurriedly went up the steps to our bedroom. My husband was dressing for work and said, 'woman, where have you been'? It was now daylight and I always went straight home from work. I opened my mouth to answer my husband but could not speak in English. I was still speaking in tongues! My husband looked at me in amazement, his eyes seemed to be bigger than ever, and he listened for a few minutes and then walked past me and left the house. He didn't come home that night and I didn't know what to think. Has he left me for good? Is my marriage over?

I was off work the next day and my cousin, Jackie, came by to have coffee with me. She asked me why I was not smoking as I usually did while drinking coffee. I said I didn't want to smoke. She then said something was different about me and I like Peter when asked if he was one of the disciples denied being different. She then exclaimed 'you're saved aren't you'? I began to cry and she asked me why I was crying. I told her how my husband had walked out without saying anything when he heard me speaking in tongues and I hadn't heard from him since. She smiled and said; 'don't worry, he'll be back. You should be happy you're saved'.

Later that evening, Jackie called and asked if I was going to attend the bingo game with the rest of my cousins that night and I said yes. She then said you're not going with me! You're saved! And she hung up the phone. Again I cried thinking to myself I've lost my husband and my family!

Chapter 19-A Greater Way of Living

Sunday morning I got the kids ready to go to my new church. I didn't know I was going to my husband's family's church. The pastor and many of the members were related to him. I had only met the relatives on his father's side and these are members on his mother's side. I was introduced to the church by the pastor who is a cousin to my husband and after the service was over, the pastor's mother came to me and asked which Phifer I was married to. I said William and she said 'you're married to Cousin Alberta's boy'. She looked at my oldest daughter and said 'she looks just like Alberta'! I felt very welcome in the church but it was dulled by my husband not being with me.

We went home after the service and later my husband came home. We discussed my salvation and he said he was used to hearing someone speak in tongues; his grandmother was saved and spoke in tongues regularly. I asked him if he would come to church with me the next Sunday and he said yes if we would go to another church. He was not ready to surrender his life to God. He had gone to church regularly with his grandmother in his youth and recognized that he needed to live holy but was not quite ready to have God change him. He felt he would lose something by surrendering and later realized he was gaining a chance for eternal life with Jesus and peace of mind during this life.

The next Sunday we went to a church pastored by the husband of a friend of mine from work. I liked the church but really wanted to go back to the church I was saved in. The holiness church I was saved in did not believe in smoking or drinking alcoholic beverages. God had already delivered me from smoking and I was not a fan of alcohol so I felt at home there.

The church my husband and I were visiting was going away with their pastor the next Sunday; but I had forgotten they would not be in town. We pulled into the parking lot which was filled with cars and got out of the car and walked to the door. The door was locked and the first thing that came to my mind was the rapture had come and we had been left behind. I then remembered the church was traveling by bus to the designated place of worship; thus the cars were in the parking lot. My husband then suggested we go to his family's church.

It was a beautiful service that morning and my husband was so touched he went to the altar and said he wanted to be baptized. This was the beginning of a new life for us. My husband did not receive the Holy Ghost that day but was delivered from smoking cigarettes and no longer had a taste for alcohol. He had prayed and asked God to take the taste of those things from him. He went back to the doctor and found out he had been healed of cirrhosis of the liver also. God was now in charge of our lives. We were committed to Him and to each other and blessings began to flow in our home.

My husband and I decided I would continue to work at the car plant. My husband had received a new confidence in me and in our marriage; but most of all his confidence was in God. It seems the women he had dated before me had cheated on him and he admitted my working with mostly men in the car plant threatened him mentally. He was still seeking to be filled with the Holy Ghost and he and my middle son went to church on a Wednesday night and both were filled with God's spirit evidenced by the speaking in tongues. **And they were all filled with the Holy Ghost, and began to speak in other tongues, as the spirit gave them utterance.** Acts 2:4

In 1985 my husband and I bought our second home; a large five bedroom, three and a half bath colonial with a backyard adjoining Mill Creek Park. We wanted a large home so the kids who lived out of town could have a place to stay when they came home to visit. God was really blessing us! My oldest son had left for the army after graduating high school and we were rearing his son, Larry Jr., who to this day is a great source of help to us. My granny became ill and instead of placing her in a nursing home my husband and I decided she would live with us. William was so patient with her and spent many an evening in her room chatting about the 'old days'. Granny had elderly neighbors that I took to doctors' appointments along with granny. The man's wife died and he had no place to go where he could be taken care of so we took him in also.

Chapter 20-The Call to Ministry

I had become a minister in our church and served as a baptismal counselor, an altar evangelist and leader of the women's assembly. My husband saw the call to ministry on my life before I did and was always supportive of anything I was doing for God and his people. I was often invited to be the speaker for prayer breakfasts and remember like it was yesterday the first time God manifested healing in one of those meetings. I had finished ministering the word and the people began to line up for me to lay hands and pray for them. This was new to me so I began to pray silently asking God 'what am I supposed to do next'? I heard the Holy Spirit speaking through me as I prayed the prayer He was giving me for each person. I didn't feel any fire in my hands as I laid hands on the different individuals. No one fell to the floor under the anointing as I had seen happen when others prayed for healing. Some of my family on my father's side was singers for Kathryn Kuhlman Ministries and we knew immediately when someone was healed. It seemed that nothing spectacular or unusual happened and I left feeling tired in my body and with the feeling that I had prayed for different healings but wondered if I prayed amiss because I saw no manifestation that healing had occurred.

A few weeks later I was shopping in an open market when a man approached me asking, 'aren't you the lady that prayed for me at the prayer breakfast'? I looked at the man and recognized him as being the person I prayed for who had a tumor on his brain. He was to have an operation the week after the prayer. He said he went into the hospital and they shaved one side of his head and took him to x-ray to mark the exact position of the tumor but the x-ray was showing the tumor was gone. God had healed the man and he was thanking me! I looked at the man and said, 'sir, all I did was pray the prayer the Holy Spirit was giving me; all the glory for your healing goes to God'.

Many healings and testimonies of the same came forth after each service and God continued to not allow me to know when He was moving; I was only required to pray the prayers he was giving me. I also hosted a Wednesday night prayer service in my home. It began with eight women and soon grew into as many as forty. I would always begin the service by asking each person for their prayer request and regardless of how many people were in the circle, God would allow me to remember each request as we prayed aloud. Now this was unusual for me because I would get the names of my own children mixed up and sometimes even call them by my siblings' names.

One night one of the elderly members asked for prayer for her family. She had no children of her own but always prayed for her nieces and nephews. When I began to pray her request it was like I was a needle on a record that had gotten stuck in one place. I continued to call out her nephew's name and asking God to cover him in His blood.

This went on for a few minutes before I felt the release to continue praying for the requests of the other members. Later that night as I was lying in bed the mother of this young man I was praying for called to say her son was in the hospital having emergency surgery; he had been shot several times. I asked if she wanted me to come to the hospital and she said, 'no, my auntie said you had already prayed for him and put a blood covering over him! I just wanted you to know he was covered in blood when they brought him in and I don't know how many times he was shot'. That was on a Wednesday night. On the following Sunday the young man was in church giving his testimony of being shot nine times and all were flesh wounds. **He had been covered in the blood of Jesus!**

In 1988 I decided I had worked outside the home long enough. My oldest son was still in the army, my second oldest was working in a meat shop and my baby boy was in college on an athletic scholarship. Four of my five children have attended private school and all have had some college experience. My oldest daughter has a Master's degree in social work and is now a licensed social worker. My youngest daughter has her Bachelor's degree and works as a communicator. My husband and I decided to buy houses to renovate and lease. We purchased nine houses and rented them out to ensure that we would be able to maintain the same standard of living as we had while I was working. The added income helped the girls and me pay for the first year of college. Yes, after leaving the car plant I decided to go back to college at the same time three of my children were there. This did not embarrass them and the girls and I sometimes did homework together. My son didn't join us because he was living on campus.

Chapter21-The Death of my Brother

In 1993 I hosted a women's conference at the church and it was centered on the necessity of prayer. One of the prayer topics was 'the prayer of relinquishment'. I assigned the prayer topics to several of the female evangelists but could not get anyone to take the prayer of relinquishment so I decided to pray it myself. As I prayed the tears began to run uncontrollably down my face as I relinquished all that I had to God including my family members. I couldn't understand why I was crying so hard while praying. The next day was Sunday and I was late for church so I didn't sit up front but sat under the balcony. I felt heavy and couldn't explain the reason for my heaviness. I don't remember hearing anything from the message. I was in church but my mind seemed to be elsewhere. I went home after service still heavy in my spirit.

It was about 3:30 in the afternoon when the phone rang. The caller was saying my youngest brother had been shot at a cousin's house when he answered her door. I asked which hospital he was taken to and they gave me the information. I then turned to the wall and began to petition God to reveal to me if my brother would live or die. God impressed upon my heart these words, 'I have given him life'. I hurriedly dressed to go to the hospital and as I walked by the surgery wing I could feel the presence of my brother. The surgery doors were open so I walked in wearing my hospital clerical badge and asked about the wounded man that had been brought in. They asked which one stabbing or shooting victim. I said shooting victim and they asked if I was a relative and I said, yes, I'm his sister. They ushered me out of the surgical suite and said a doctor would come out to talk to me. I joined several family members who were in the waiting room and waited for the doctor.

Several doctors and nurses came out about five minutes later to say my brother had died on the operating table. I asked to see him but had to wait until they cleaned him up. Finally, they allowed us to go into the room and my brother lay there with one tear in his eye. We were at a catholic hospital and they sent a priest down to pray for us. I thanked the priest for coming but told him I wanted to pray for my family. In the prayer, I thanked God for the forty-two years my brother had lived, and then relinquished him to God. I now know why none of the other evangelists could pray that prayer. The God who is the author and finisher of our faith; and knows our end before our beginning, was preparing me for what was to come. My cousin had been in a fight the day before and the person she was fighting sent two of her relatives to shoot her. My brother was in the wrong place at the wrong time or was he in the right place at the right time? God's word to me was he had given my brother life! My brother had been baptized and received the Holy Ghost in my home some months earlier. Our God is an awesome God!

Chapter 22-Heartbreaking Ministry

In 1996 I was scheduled to have surgery but was delaying it because I had no one to care for granny. The gentleman I had taken care of had passed the year before and my only choice was to put her in a nursing home temporarily. My children had all moved away and my husband was working with an engineering unit which traveled the east coast. Every year in September our church, under the leadership of the late Bishop N.L. Wagner, hosted a conference called Pentecost in Perspective or PIP. I decided I would wait until PIP was over to place granny in the nursing home. I always opened my home to delegates from the different countries that needed a place to stay and this particular year I was to host twin sisters from England.

PIP was to start on Wednesday and on Monday I received a call to pray for an uncle who had fallen down his stairs apparently while suffering a stroke. I began praying for him when I got a call from my oldest son saying he had been having very bad headaches. He was stationed in Tacoma, Washington at the time. I urged him to get to the hospital immediately because I, too, had been having pain in my head; but the doctors couldn't find the cause for the pain. Reluctantly my son went to the hospital and his blood pressure was so high it had blown his kidneys. I tried to make arrangements right away to go to Tacoma by placing my grandmother in the nursing home and looking for a place for the twins to stay. The members of our church were always willing to take in delegates but everyone's home was already filled. I wanted to get to my son as soon as possible.

The doctor from the veteran's hospital called me to tell me my son's condition and said they were keeping him heavily sedated while trying to lower his blood pressure. My son was in ICU and I asked the doctor if he could bring in a phone and put it to my son's ear so I could pray for him. The doctor had a nurse bring in a phone and I prayed for my son and told him I would be there tomorrow which was Tuesday. Meanwhile my pastor and his staff prayed for my son. I was unable to get a flight out on the next day and still had not found a place for the twins.

PIP started on Wednesday and I was up late on Tuesday night explaining to the twins the purpose of the baptism in Jesus name and how it miraculously eradicates us of our sins; when we go down in the watery grave we come up new and clean in God's eyes. I dropped the twins off before breakfast at the church and they were baptized in Jesus name and received the gift of the Holy Ghost, I felt my assignment was over but my pastor was saying it was not time for me to leave yet. A woman who was on dialysis and in need of a kidney transplant was coming to PIP. She had made arrangements to have dialysis in her hotel room and she believed by faith that God would heal her. Thursday night my pastor had her come to the altar and called his wife, one of the conference speakers, and me to pray for her. Surely, I thought, my assignment is over now. Well the twins didn't leave until Saturday and I was able to get a flight to Seattle, Washington Saturday morning. My son's girlfriend met me at SeaTac airport and drove me to the hospital to see my son. When he heard my voice he told the nurse, 'I told you my mother would be here today'. My son thought it was Tuesday because I told him on Monday that I would be there tomorrow. It was actually four days later!

My son needed to have dialysis and I was in the room with him for his first treatment. Seeing my son's blood going through a tube from his body into the dialysis machine and back into his body made me weak in the knees. I told my son I needed to use the restroom and went there and cried like a baby. God is good and I soon gathered enough composure to return to the room and make small talk with my son. He was released from the hospital but would have dialysis treatments at his home. I was with my son for about a week when I started having chest pains. I enquired of the Lord if it were my pain or if I were to pray for someone else. The Lord ensured me it was not my pain so I prayed for whoever it was that was in distress. The pain left and I fell asleep and was awakened by a phone call from my oldest daughter saying, 'granny has died and the nursing home needs to know where to send her body'. I gave my daughter the instructions and then got on the phone to change my airline ticket. I wanted to get home as soon as possible to make arrangements for her burial.

God always makes a way of provision in the time of need! When I returned home I went to the funeral home and found that my cousins, Ray and Carolyn, had already gone to the funeral home and paid for the funeral! To God be given the glory for the great things he had done.

My oldest son wanted to move back to Youngstown so we began to make preparations for his brothers to pack up his house and drive him home. He was placed on a list to receive a kidney transplant and I was eagerly awaiting it.

In 2000 I was privileged to travel with Bishop Wagner and his wife Lady Rita to Paris, France, through Switzerland by train and on to Milan, Italy where I was able to teach the word of God.

In 2002 the call came for my son to have a transplant and my son was reluctant about surgery. He felt in his spirit that something would go wrong. My son was now very thin and his skin was always dry from the fluid being removed by dialysis. I wanted him to have the kidney transplant because it could give him a new lease on life. He had the transplant and was to be released from the hospital when his stomach became enlarged and the doctors discovered his intestine had been perforated. My husband and I rushed to the hospital as they were taking my son to surgery.

The surgery seemed to last for hours. A dear friend of mine happened to be the surgical nurse in the operating room that night. She also is a woman of prayer. After the surgery was over the doctor came out to tell me my son would most likely not make it through the night. I thanked him for his medical knowledge but told him he was not God. He retorted, 'thank you for that information', and walked away. I left my family in the waiting room and went to the chapel of the catholic hospital we were in and fell prostrate before the Lord. I said to God, 'I know Larry does not belong to me: you only lent him to me and you have the right to take him back; but you promised not to take anyone from my family without them being saved and Larry is not saved'! I then felt the Lord impress upon my heart to stand up and praise him! I got up off the floor and lifted my hands toward heaven with tears streaming down my face as I worshipped God. I had entered the chapel alone but when I opened my eyes there were several people standing and watching me. I didn't allow that to hinder my worship but continued until I felt a release from the Lord. I walked out the chapel and there was my son's doctor coming out of the cafeteria. He looked at me and said, 'your son is holding his own, you keep doing what you're doing and I'll do all I can to help him'. It may seem odd but just recalling this information makes it seem like it was yesterday when this actually happened fifteen years ago.

Larry went through many surgical procedures and left the hospital after several weeks with a large opening in his stomach with a mesh covering it. You could literally see his intestines when changing his bandages. My nurse friend told me later that much of his intestines had died and when the surgeon touched it, it would crumble; she didn't think they would have enough intestines to hook to the colon for normal activity. The colon was blackened and appeared to be dysfunctional. Larry had to go through many washings of his intestine to try to fight off bacteria. During his second surgery it was discovered that the colon had turned back to its normal color. God is great and greatly to be praised!

We had many scares of losing Larry during this time. On one occasion I was getting ready to leave for Columbus, Ohio to minister when I received a call to come to the hospital because Larry was very ill. I prayed before leaving home to find out from God what I should do and my answer from God was: 'you take care of my business and I'll take care of your son'! In the meantime my husband was urging me to go forth and minister and he would stay with Larry. I stopped by the hospital and prayed with Larry and then went on to Columbus. There was a great outpouring during the altar call and many were healed of their infirmities.

Before leaving from Columbus for home I was taken to a store and purchased a picture of 'Footprints' for my son's home. I wanted him to be able to see how God was carrying him during his illness. I drove back to Youngstown the next day and went straight to the hospital to see Larry. He seemed to be in a good spirit as he told me of a visitor he had while I was away.

A foreign doctor who was not part of the team which usually took care of Larry came in wearing a turban on his head and asked Larry who ordered him to be washed out in surgery? Larry answered the doctor by saying I don't know who ordered it. The strange doctor then said; 'you're not to be washed in surgery again'. Larry said the doctor had a can with a syringe attached to it which he inserted in Larry's rectum. He then wrote something on Larry's chart. The regular doctor came in to prepare Larry for surgery and read the chart and asked my son which doctor wrote the new order. **Could this possibly have been another angel?** My son said he had never seen this doctor before. My son was never taken to surgery to wash his intestines again.

Even though Larry had received the new kidney they were still using dialysis on him. It was my birthday and I was asking God for two things;

1. I wanted Larry off dialysis
2. I wanted to pass the test to receive my real estate license

I took my test and passed with a high score and headed for the hospital to see Larry. He was not in his room; he had been taken to have dialysis. I was very upset as I walked to the dialysis room. My son's kidney doctor was in the process of hooking him up to the machine as I walked into the room. I spoke with authority from God that the kidney would not work if they kept putting him on dialysis. The doctor was startled at the sound in my voice and said: 'I believe you're right' and unhooked my son. The kidney began to work and Larry never had dialysis again. Our God is a healer and can deliver us from anything!

Larry was released from the hospital after spending several months there. He had a colostomy bag and was told he would need one for the rest of his life because his intestine was short and to hook it to his colon could cause complications. Larry had the bag for one year and was able to be hooked up normally again. He was on anti-rejection medications for the new kidney but was able to get around well and enjoy his life again. I was relieved but the stress of his illness had caused physical damage in my body.

It was the last week of 2003 and I was scheduled for a visit with my doctor. I was experiencing shortness of breath and tired easily, especially when trying to shop for groceries. My skin tone had changed and become darker with a gray cast to it. I had no insurance because my husband had retired in 1998 and I was not old enough for Medicare, so my appointment was at a clinic. I walked into the cubicle at the clinic and my doctor took one look at me and said she wanted to do an EKG. The EKG came back revealing nothing but because Dr. Gwendolyn Hughes felt something was wrong she insisted on calling a cardiologist. I protested because I didn't have money for a specialist, but she said he owed her a favor. I thank Dr. Hughes for intervening for me.

Dr. Hughes knew I was a person who believed in prayer and she heard me tell of the miracles God had performed in the life of my son. Prior to this visit she had asked me to pray for her nurse who was diagnosed with throat cancer and scheduled to have surgery. I was humbled by Dr. Hughes request and it was hard to hold back the tears as I asked the nurse to come into my cubicle and then asked for permission to pray for her. She consented and I began to pray while simultaneously asking God for specifics to pray for. I heard in my spirit God saying: "pray the cancer be capsulized"! I didn't understand what that meant but prayed those words in obedience. Several weeks later, on my next doctor's visit, I asked how the nurse was doing and they thought I knew she had the surgery and was back at work. The cancer was enclosed in a capsule-like bubble and they were able to get it out without rupturing it. The nurse and my doctor came in to thank me. The nurse kept saying; 'it's all because of you Ms. Joyce, it's all because of you and your prayer'! I quickly told them all the glory goes to God! I only prayed the prayer he gave me!

Dr. Hughes made the call to her friend, the cardiologist, and I was scheduled to go into the hospital to have a heart catheterization. It revealed 90% blockage in the main artery and 70% blockages in two other arteries. I was told if I had a heart attack I would be dead before I hit the floor. They wanted to send me to surgery immediately. I believe in being covered by prayer before one has any type of surgical procedure and the next night was New Year's Eve and I wanted to be in service so my pastor and church could pray for me. I spoke my concern to the doctor and the heart surgery was scheduled for January 3, 2004.

I went home as soon as they released me and informed my children and family members of the upcoming surgery. New Years' service was wonderful and the pastor and church prayed for me. I was use to receiving prayer directives from the pastor for others, but this was the first time I had one given for me. The pastor had the prayer warriors sign a paper showing the individual hour that each person praying was to take. He then spoke words that sent a chill through my body; 'don't let her die on your watch'! One of my closest friends told me she prayed for me during the entire procedure but didn't sign the prayer paper because if I died she was not going to have the pastor scold her. We laugh about it today because the pastor was adamant about what he said. I ended up having a quadruple by-pass instead of the triple by-pass and all went well! To God be the glory for the great things he has done. I must interject another blessing. The day before my surgery a young woman called saying she was to have a lumpectomy on her breast. The doctors had found a large suspicious lump there. She was to go to the same hospital to have her procedure and it was to be done on the same day as my procedure. She asked if she could come by my house for prayer. I didn't tell her of my dilemma, I simply prayed for her. She didn't have to have the procedure because they could no longer find the lump! She was shocked when she found out later that I had open-heart surgery on that same day. What an awesome God we serve.

In May of 2004 I was asked by the CEO of the clinic to participate in a panel discussion about the benefits of health clinics with President George Bush, the CEO, Dr. Ronald Dwinnels, and several of the board members of the clinic. This event, which was held at Youngstown State University, was broadcast nationwide. I was asked how long ago I had surgery. I praised God for it being in January; President Bush shouted 'hallelujah' and the newspaper took a picture of President Bush rejoicing with me.

I was later asked to become a board member of the clinic and remained in that position until 2014. My husband and I were invited to a Christmas dinner at the White House by President and Lady Bush in December of 2004. There must have been about eight hundred guests and I felt blessed to be in attendance. Each guest had the opportunity to take a picture with the president and his wife. We waited in line as a member of the armed forces took down our name to announce us to the president. I was surprised by the president as I stood next to be called; the president didn't wait for my introduction but instead introduced me himself saying, 'Joyce Phifer from Youngstown, Ohio'. I later told one of his aides that I was surprised the president remembered me. The aide said it could be years from now and the president might ask; I wonder how Joyce Phifer in Youngstown is doing? I found President Bush to be very personable. I've often wondered why I was there but could it be God sending me there to in some way to prepare for the arrival of President Obama?

In July of 2004 I was honored with an honorary Doctor of Ministry from I.A.U.G.T. International Apostolic University of Grace and Truth. This achievement for my works in ministry is very dear to my heart and I am grateful to Dr. Gloria Forward and her board for bestowing this great honor on me. I was blessed to teach at the university and also brought students from my 'School of Prayer and Intercession' to help them begin their work in ministry. I continued teaching throughout the next eight years.

January 2010 brought about a great change in my life when my pastor, Bishop Norman L. Wagner, went to be with the Lord. It was a great shock to the congregation because his death was unexpected. He had heart surgery and was home recuperating and we believed all was well. I received a call to pray for him and then a call saying he had died. I remember falling to my knees to pray when I received the first call. It was as if heaven had closed its doors to my prayer. It seemed my words were hitting the ceiling of my living room and falling back down to me. I had experienced silence before when attempting to override the will of God in prayer, but never had I experienced heaven closing to my prayer. I then knew I would have to accept the will of God. My pastor, confident, and friend would no longer be available to me in this life.

In 2013 my Larry was stricken with cancer and in 2014 he began to deteriorate, he no longer had an appetite and did not tell me the cancer had spread to his head even though he shared it with a friend. My son Coya called me to say how worried he was about Larry and he wanted him to go to the hospital but Larry refused. I went to talk to him and he said he was not ready to go to the hospital but promised he would go by week's end. I held him to his promise and took him to the hospital. He seemed better after a few days and said he had called me to take him home but I wouldn't answer the phone. The truth is he never called but was hallucinating. Mother's Day came and I spent the entire day at the hospital. Larry was now unable to communicate with us. I went back to the chapel in the hospital to ask God's will in the matter and this time there was only silence. I felt in my spirit God was going to take him.

I returned to his room and whispered in my son's ear that it was alright for him to go. It may seem strange but knowing the will of God made it easier for me to release my son. We made arrangements for him to come home on Monday for his last days but before daylight on Monday he breathed his last breath. I sat by his lifeless body and thanked God for giving us 12 more years after the doctor said he probably would not make it through the night. My child is now safe with his creator.

I moved in March of 2014 from an apartment into a house next to my son Coya to help him, as a single father of two, with his children. For about 30 days I would hear a shofar blowing around the same time each evening. Each time it would blast seven times. One night it was so loud I thought someone was standing beneath my bedroom window blowing it. You may be asking the question, 'what is a shofar'? A shofar is an instrument mentioned in the Bible. It is a trumpet originally made of a ram's horn and used by the ancient Hebrews. Many churches are now using the shofar in their services. The Hebrews would blow the shofar for many different reasons inclusive of, but not limited to:

    1. To signify the arrival of a dignitary

    2. To call the people to assemble

    3. When someone died

4. for special ceremonies

5. A call to war

God was preparing me for the death of my child. I was not the only one to hear the shofar. My husband and daughter heard it also. Later, we found out that the people who live next door have a van they used for their church and it has a horn with the sound of a shofar. Why it blasted at the same time every night for those 30 days they could not explain because no one would be in the van at the time the horn was blasting.

I spend my time in preparation of the rapture. My soul must be ready and I must help others to get ready. It won't matter if I die before he comes because the grave will not hold me back. The promise is: those who die in Christ will rise first, and then those who are alive will meet them in the air. One way or another I rise. Someone posed this question to me. What if the Bible is a fallacy? You will have lived your life in vain. I smiled and said; my belief has kept me from desiring to do wrong, it has caused me to love others as I want to be loved, it has taught me to forgive others because I want to be forgiven, it has given me joy, peace and hope, it has caused me to live life on purpose, that purpose has been to help others come out of sin and darkness to have a better life. So even if it was a fallacy and it isn't, I still would have the victory!

Division Four-Rapture Season

Chapter 23-Come to Jesus

Now you may have wondered why I chose to write about an ancient Jewish wedding. The Jewish wedding parallels with the upcoming rapture. The groom in the story goes home to prepare a place for his bride. Our groom, Jesus, went home to prepare a place for us. The groom in the story could not return for his bride until his father said' it is now ready'! We cannot be raptured until our heavenly Father says to Jesus 'it is now ready'! Throughout the Bible God has used weddings in illustration of his desire to see man and woman come together as one in him. We come into the world searching for happiness and we look for it most often in the wrong places. Mankind is always in pursuit of love, approval, success and happiness. Could we be looking for these things because we have an inner inkling of what it was like before we left Heaven? Please understand, God is not against us succeeding in life. Joshua 1:8 reads thusly, **This book of the law shall not depart out of thy mouth; but thou shat meditate therin day and night that thou mayest observe to do according to all that is written therein: for then thou shalt make thy way prosperous, and then thou shalt have good** *success.* 3 John 2; *Beloved, I wish above all things that thou mayest prosper and be in health, even as thy soul propereth*. It is only when we desire things more than we desire God that we go astray. We can do things in the wrong way and have

success, but that type of success usually brings misery with it. Jesus wants us to desire him and be successful doing things according to the word of God. There is life after death. *Father, I will that they also, whom thou hast given me, be with me where I am; that they may behold my glory, which thou hast given me, for thou lovest me before the foundation of the world.* John 17:24. *Then shall the dust return to the earth as it was: and the spirit return to God who gave it.* Eccl. 2:7. We came from God, we belong to God, and what we are searching for is God! We are searching for the day we will become his bride. He will not divorce us. He will take us home to live with him. I don't think I will be looking back at the house I will be leaving because I will be too awed by being in the presence of my groom, the Lord Jesus Christ! I will behold him as my King.

For many years I looked down on myself for being a sinner and for having children out of wedlock. I truly believed God had forgiven me but I had a hard time forgiving myself. Please, don't misunderstand, my children are precious to me, but they never belonged to me. They are a gift from God that adds pleasure to my life. My children are jewels God lent me to nurture and love. It is my responsibility to lead them to the right path of life. They came through me but they belong to God.

You may be going through life remembering your own ungodliness and God wants you to know that nothing you

have done has caused him to stop loving you. You may have committed murder; you may have sold drugs or been a woman beater or a man beater. You may have aborted children or caused someone to have an abortion. You may be the doctor who performed the procedure and have felt guilty ever since. You may have lived a life of sexual perverseness or you may have lied, cheated or been a thief. It is God's will that **_all_** be saved because all of us have been sinners. Contrary to popular beliefs there are no big sins and little sins. Telling a 'white' lie is as offensive to God as committing murder. Yet, He forgives us the moment we ask for forgiveness and make a turn from our wicked ways. Our being baptized is an outward sign of an inward work. Receiving the Holy Ghost is the fulfillment of the gift God promised us. His word says that all who believe in him shall be saved. He died for you and me. He took our sins to the cross when he shed his blood for us.

Today we often times attend churches that teach us how to become rich; some teach us life skills, some others may teach us how to have good relationships and other good things and I am not against any of this. My mission is to let others know of the soon coming of our Lord in the rapture. I, too, started out as a young woman in pursuit of natural things. I wanted beautiful cars and God allowed me to own three different Lincolns, and a couple of other luxury cars. I wanted a beautiful house and God gave me one. I desired beautiful clothing and jewelry and God supplied those things also. One day as I was in a funeral procession of a well to do person, it dawned on me that no one takes those material things to the grave. There is no moving van filled with worldly treasures following the hearse. This scripture then came in my thoughts: **Lay not up for yourselves treasures upon the earth, where moth and rust doth corrupt, and where thieves break through and** *steal: but lay up for yourself treasures in heaven, where neither moth nor rust doth corrupt, and where thieves do not break through and steal: for where your treasure is there will your heart be also.* Matthew 6:19-21.

I began this book by saying what a miracle life is and on February 20, 2017, I experienced the birth of my great grand-daughter, Kennedy, who was born on president's day. I, along with her father, watched as she emerged through the birth canal of her mother and entered into life. What an experience! Joy filled the room as we heard her first cry. God had sent forth a new life for her parents and extended family to nourish, provide for, and guide towards eternal life with Jesus. I am so grateful for the opportunity to help her parents in the rearing of this precious child; she is a miracle from God! It is my desire to prepare her for the arrival of our soon coming king that she may be part of the wedding feast.

Chapter 24-The Greatest Wedding

We are living in the time of the greatest wedding that has ever been seen by mankind. We are about to experience a wedding of royalty, a wedding of grandeur, and a wedding more prominent and meaningful than any wedding that has ever occurred, a wedding that has been in the mind of God before the foundation of the world. The bride's groom is Jesus, our Lord and Savior, and soon coming King. The bride is the people who love Him, men, women, boys and girls of every creed and nation, black, white, yellow and red; all who love Jesus and believe in him will be part of the bride. God has a plan to rapture us!

What I like about the Father's plan for mankind is this. I don't have to worry about dying and being left behind. I Thessalonians 4:16-17; **For the Lord himself shall descend from Heaven with a shout, with the voice of the archangel, and with the voice of God: and the dead in Christ shall rise first: Then we which are alive and remain shall be caught up together with them in the clouds, to meet the Lord in the air: and so shall we ever be with the Lord.**

I can visualize the Lord coming down from Heaven on the cloud. I hear the trump of God! I see the graves opening up and souls coming forth that have been transformed into their new bodies. The new bodies will never again experience sickness, pain, heartbreak or death. They are coming up from every graveyard in every nation, on every continent; from Asia, Australia, and Antarctica, they are coming up from the seas and the oceans. I see them coming from North America, South America, Europe and Africa and all of their garments have been made white.

Meanwhile on earth there are trains wrecking, airplanes are falling, cars and buses crash, there is a shut-down in factories, hospitals and businesses as those who are alive and remain receive their new bodies and join the King in the air. Yes, we, the people of God are in awe as we meet our Lord, Savior and King. He is majestic in his robe of glory and we now behold him face to face.

The cloud is lifted up into Heaven where the people of God get to see the mansions that have been prepared for them, joy is in the air, and there is a feeling of peace, safety and real love as we enter our new homes. Homes we didn't have to build, clothes we didn't pay for, yet, everything we need is waiting for us. A great wedding feast is being laid out before us as we celebrate our Lord. The celebration seems to go on forever and God's people are in awe of his majesty. The beauty of Heaven is so glorious and everywhere you look the sight is breathtaking. There is no more sorrow or even a thought of what was left behind. Sounds of Worship are everywhere as God's people give Him glory and honor. Family members who were lame are there but they are no longer lame! There are no crutches or wheelchairs in Heaven. Those who were crippled on earth are now standing tall as they worship the Lord. I see those who were blind during my lifetime and they are able to see! There is no cancer, no diabetes, no hypertension or any other kind of illness there. I meet the apostles and Moses and even Hannah! I see the twelve gates, the Crystal Lake and the golden streets. I marvel at all that I see and yet what I see is minute in the magnitude of Heaven and all of its glory. People recognize me and I recognize them even though we have new bodies. Oh, the awesomeness of this place and of our God. The angels are singing of his glory and we bow to Him in great reverence.

However on earth there is great sorrow, men and women are weeping because they didn't believe this could even happen. They saw the Bible as being a book of fairy tales. They never took salvation literally. They believed we evolved by evolution. I can hear the sobbing and the cry 'why didn't somebody tell me Jesus is real?' I didn't believe, I just didn't believe! **Behold, I stand at the door; and knock: if any man hear my voice, and open the door, I will come in to him, and will sup with him, and he with me. Rev. 3:20.** The gospel had been preached on television and internet as well as in the church. Tent meetings had been set up in remote areas so everyone could have a chance to hear the word of the Lord, we have no excuse. Husbands are sobbing because their wives were taken up. Wives who begged their husbands to get right with God. Mothers of small children are seeing them fly out of their arms and off their laps because the children being innocent have been raptured. Young teens that have been rebellious are seeing their parents being caught up, parents who taught them the word of God, but they refused to accept the teachings of salvation and are now on their knees as they see their mothers, fathers, sisters and brothers who believed, meet the Lord in the air.

And if it seem evil to you to serve the Lord, choose you this day whom ye will serve; whether the gods whom your fathers served that were on the other side of the flood, or the gods of the Amorites, in whose land you dwell: but as for me and my house, we will serve the Lord. Joshua 23:15

Hope to meet you in the rapture!

www.ingramcontent.com/pod-product-compliance
Lightning Source LLC
Chambersburg PA
CBHW071705040426
42446CB00011B/1931